Lesser Known Fly Fishing Venues in South Park

by Michele White, owner Tumbling Trout Fly Shop

Lake George, Colorado

www.tumblingtrout.com   --- (720) 363-2092

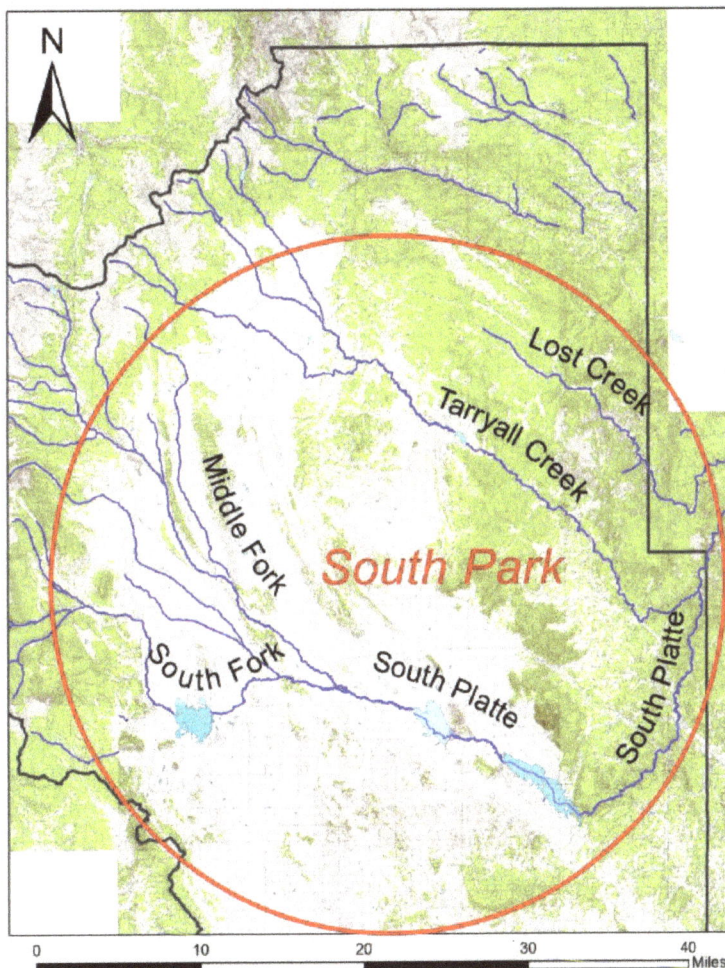

Booklet cost: $30

For my Bun because he makes life good.

Tumbling Trout Fly Shop (720) 363-2092

TABLE OF CONTENTS

FORWARD

The intention of this atlas is to relieve some of the daily fishing pressure that exists at the better known fly fishing venues: Dream Stream and Eleven Mile Canyon. Many anglers visit South Park to experience fishing our Gold Medal Waters (Charlie Myers State Wildlife Area, aka, "Dream Stream" and "Eleven Mile Canyon"). That said, there are four reservoirs in South Park with inlets and spillways and four major tributaries that comprise the South Platte River in the basin of South Park. The water above the reservoirs is recharged through run-off from the surrounding mountains and through springs and aquifers near the surface in the alluvial basin. The significance of the wild headwaters is that you can find wild resident trout year-round above the reservoirs.

When people come into my fly shop, I try to find out what their goal is for the day. Do they want to catch a grand big fish? Many fish? A variety of trout species? A shot at cutthroats? Pike? Are they fishing with a group of people? Do they have children or a dog? Would they like to hike or do they need to park next to a river? (Do they want to spin-fish, use bait, or keep a trout?) South Park offers multiple venues for a variety of fishing methods in South Park.

Prior to opening this shop, I was a geologist and GIS operator, which means I make maps using software. The back of my shop has a wall devoted to maps showing people where they are, orienting them to the region and the flow of the South Platte River, and showing a variety of options for their day. My maps have personal notes and colored lines drawn on them. People capture images of my maps using their cells phones. I began to realize that these maps in booklet form would be useful in diverting anglers to the Lesser Know Fly Fishing Venues of South Park.

Michele White, owner Tumbling Trout Fly Shop, Lake George, Colorado

NOTE: There are also public access fishing areas between Fairplay and Hoosier Pass up towards Alma, and also between Como and Boreas Pass. There are also 4WD roads to creeks. I didn't include them in this book because the South Park Basin seems to be an acceptable driving distance for people coming up for the afternoon. The trout species in the higher elevation headwaters include native cutthroat and brookies.

The Lesser Known Fly Fishing Venues in South Park

1) Lake George area

2) Tarryall River

3) Lost Creek

4) Tomahawk

5) Above Spinney (Badger Basin)

6) Wild Headwaters

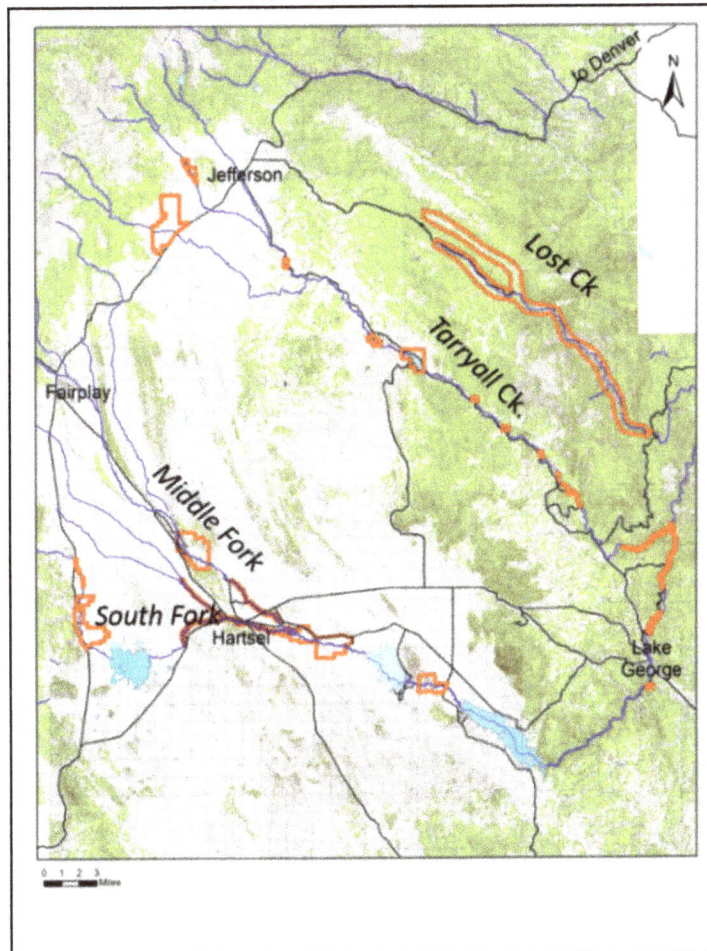

Map: Overview of Public Fishing Access in South Park Basin.

LAKE GEORGE AREA

LAKE GEORGE AREA

- Bottom Spillway (South Platte)
- Twin Creek (South Platte)
- Happy Meadows (South Platte)
- Platte Springs Triangle (Tarryall River)

BOTTOM SPILLWAY AND TWIN CREEK

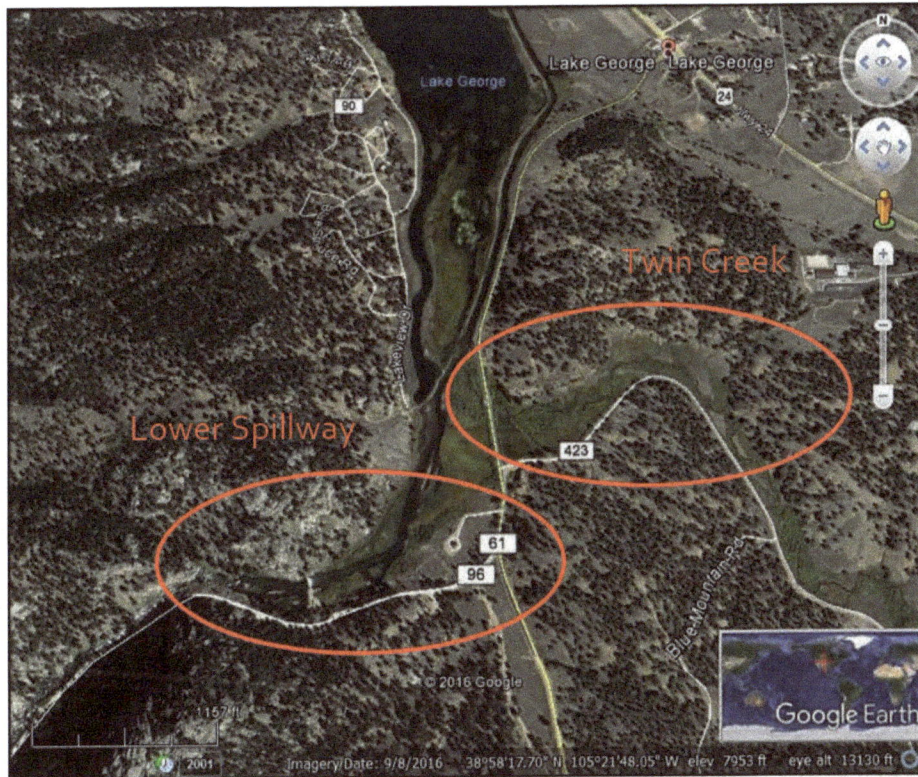

Just outside the town of Lake George, the **Bottom Spillway** (left) is before the entrance to the canyon. **Twin Creek** (right) is across from the entrance to the canyon. The bottom spillway is a dam that impedes trout from migrating up or downstream. In the fall , you can watch large brown trout try to leap up the spillway. There is a wading trail that goes up into the canyon from this parking lot. You can fish both above or below the dam for large trout that cannot migrate beyond this barrier.

4

The Bottom Spillway (closed in winter until July)

Twin Creek is a small, willow lined creek that holds trout during run-off (spring and early summer).

Twin Creek

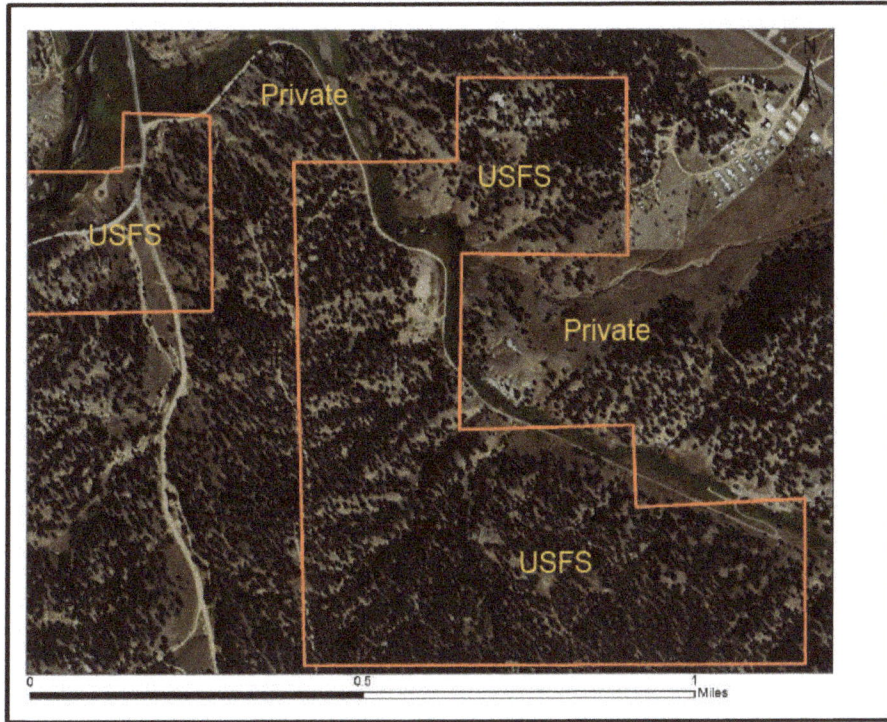

Public and private boundaries at Twin Creek are checker-board but well-marked.

HAPPY MEADOWS

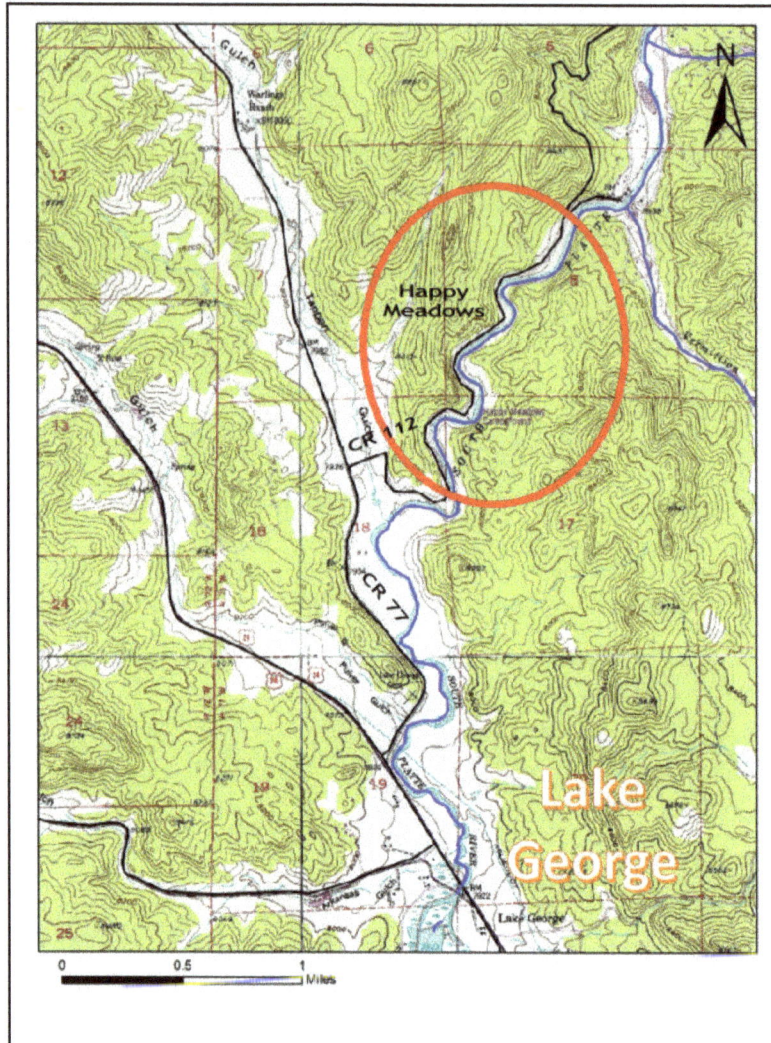

From Lake George heading west on Hwy 24, take the first right (CR 77). Then, in 2 miles take the next right (CR 112). This leads to a 2 mile stretch of public access on the South Platte River.

Happy Meadows is located between two private fishing communities – the private lake of Lake George upstream and Sportsman's Paradise downstream. You can park alongside the river. Best fishing is in rocky zones. Stocked rainbow trout and wild predatory brown trout migrate through here. This venue is heavily used in summer between 9 a.m. and 5 p.m. Spring and fall is ideal, or after sundown are best times to fish. It's a good place to take dogs because you can cross the river easily and the steep canyon walls keeps the dogs nearby but off the road. Novice fisherman can likely catch trout here because of the stocked fish. It is not uncommon to catch an 18" brown or even pike on a streamer here. (That's why it's called, "*Happy*"…)

PLATTE SPRINGS TRIANGLE (SOUTH PLATTE/TARRYALL RIVER CONFLUENCE)

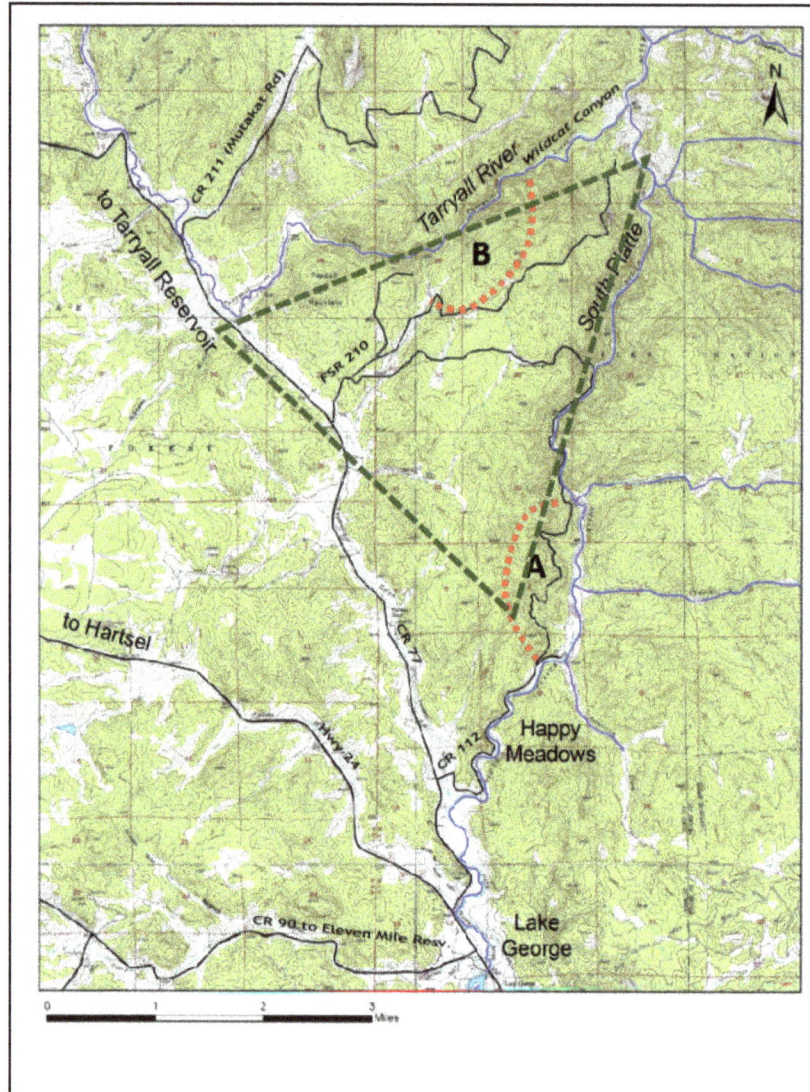

Map showing hiking routes (A and B) to both rivers.

Platte Springs Triangle: CR77 and the confluence of the Tarryall and South Platte rivers form a triangle of USFS land that is only accessible on foot. There are 2 hiking options to access either the **Tarryall in Wild Cat Canyon** or the **South Platte River** and their mutual confluence.

Route A is the Platte River Trailhead from Happy Meadows, which is about 3 miles of hiking through the woods to bypass a private fishing community. It leads to the South Platte River. The confluence with the Tarryall is another 3 miles (5 miles total to the confluence).

Route B is a system of foot trails that lead down from multiple Forest Service roads. You can either hike (difficult) on the Platte Springs Trail from FSR 210 down to the South Platte, or you can scramble down from FSR 610 to the Tarryall River. The exposure to water is limited by steep canyon. Both rivers cut through canyons, which are difficult to wade.

The confluence of the Tarryall and South Platte leads downstream through steep terrain, which is seriously inaccessible. Motorized access by 4WD is illegal though the gates have been vandalized.

Trout in this stretch include wild browns and errant stocked rainbows - large ones are whoppers.

Tarryall River in Wild Cat Canyon

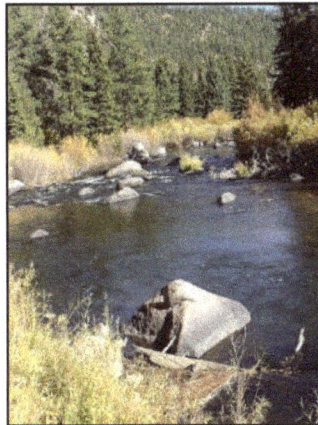

South Platte River below Platte Springs Trailhead

TARRYALL RIVER

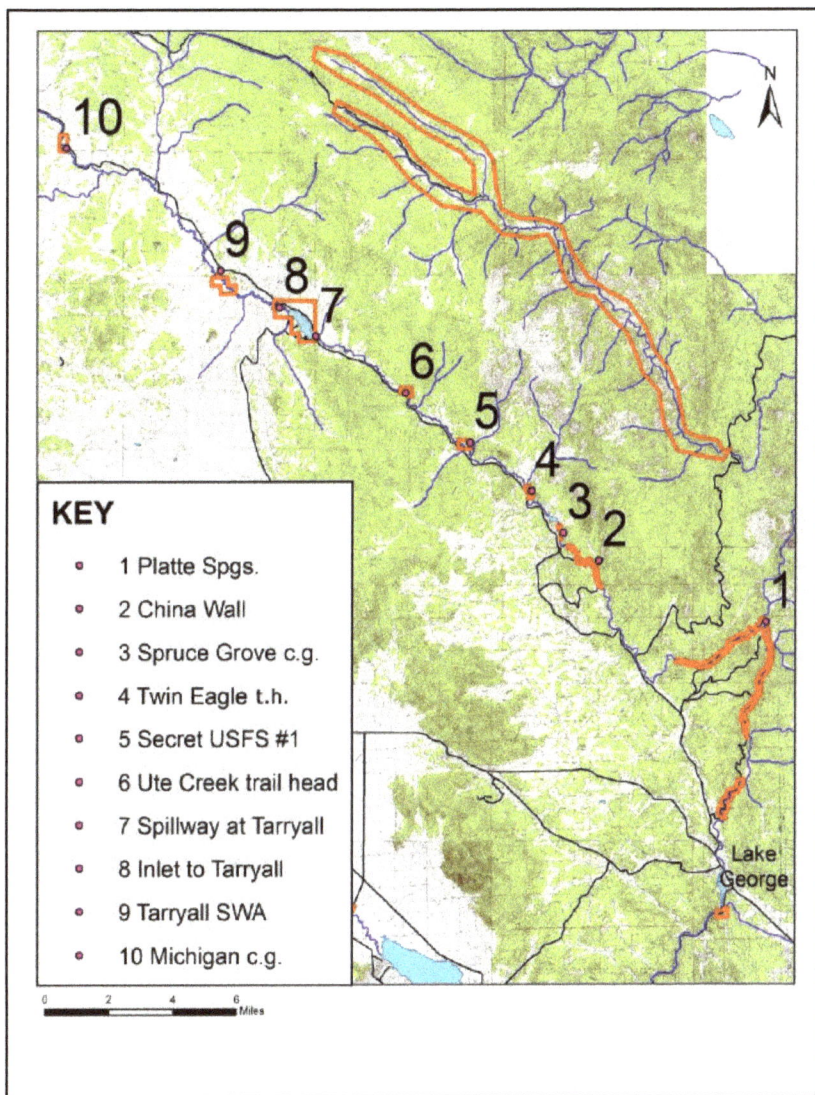

KEY

- 1 Platte Spgs.
- 2 China Wall
- 3 Spruce Grove c.g.
- 4 Twin Eagle t.h.
- 5 Secret USFS #1
- 6 Ute Creek trail head
- 7 Spillway at Tarryall
- 8 Inlet to Tarryall
- 9 Tarryall SWA
- 10 Michigan c.g.

0 2 4 6
Miles

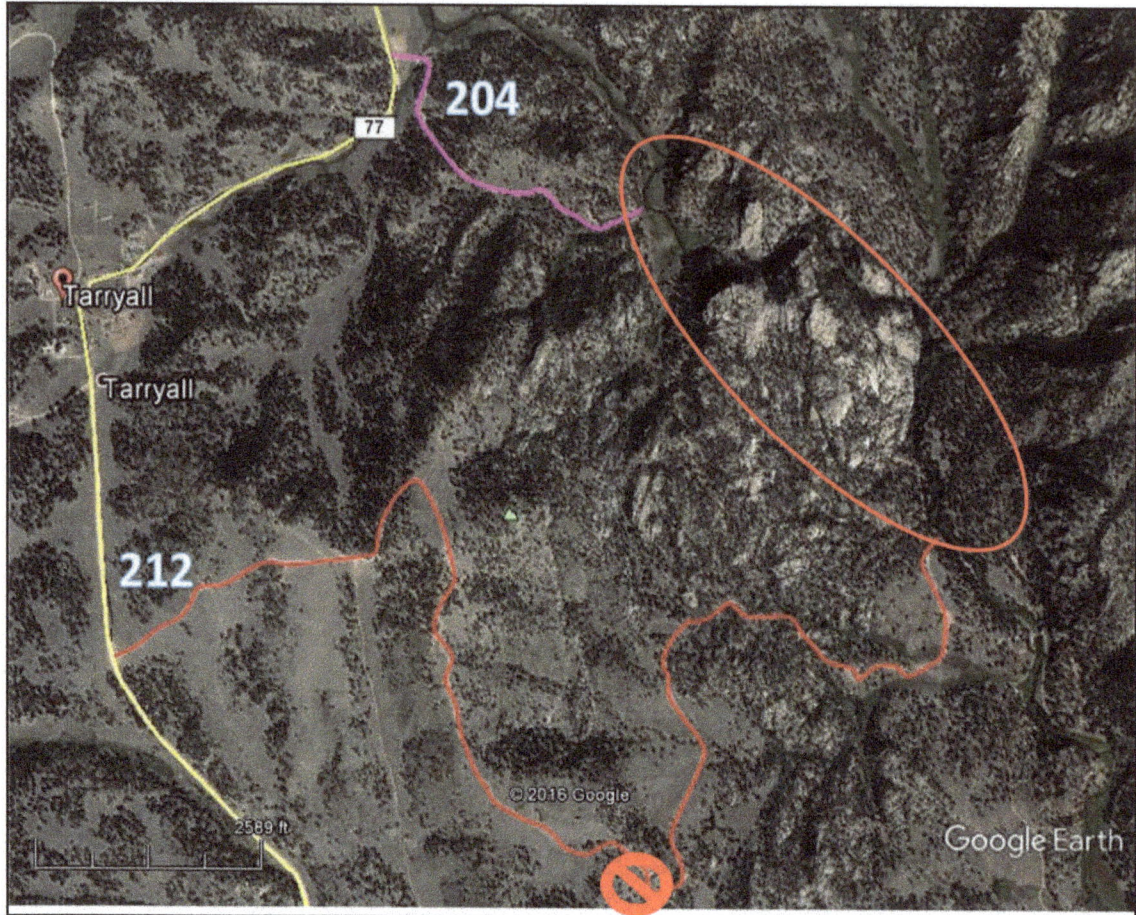

There are two accesses to **China Wall** canyon (so named because the granite forms a steep, cliff, like a wall). Both accesses are marked with identical entrance signs. The first access (coming from Lake George - FSR 212) is a rough road and a long hike; The second access (FSR 204) comes after passing through the town of Tarryall. This second access is steep but you do not need 4WD. A Subaru can do it. You can drive to the river. The foot trail along the Tarryall through the canyon is beautiful. (Open July 1 – Dec. 31)

The China Wall foot path goes between huge boulders. There are not only pools, but there are also sandy islands and willow-lined areas. Mostly 9" to 14" browns, intermittent larger predatory fish in deep pools.

Just past the town of Tarryall (and past China Wall), is a long white fence. This private property bounds between the China Wall and the **Spruce Grove Campground**. You can day park at the campground and fish down through a gorge to the white fence. Most people don't fish the gorge because the wading is tricky. This is a good place to catch abundant smaller fish because of structure and vegetation. The holes behind boulders in the gorge hold larger brown trout.

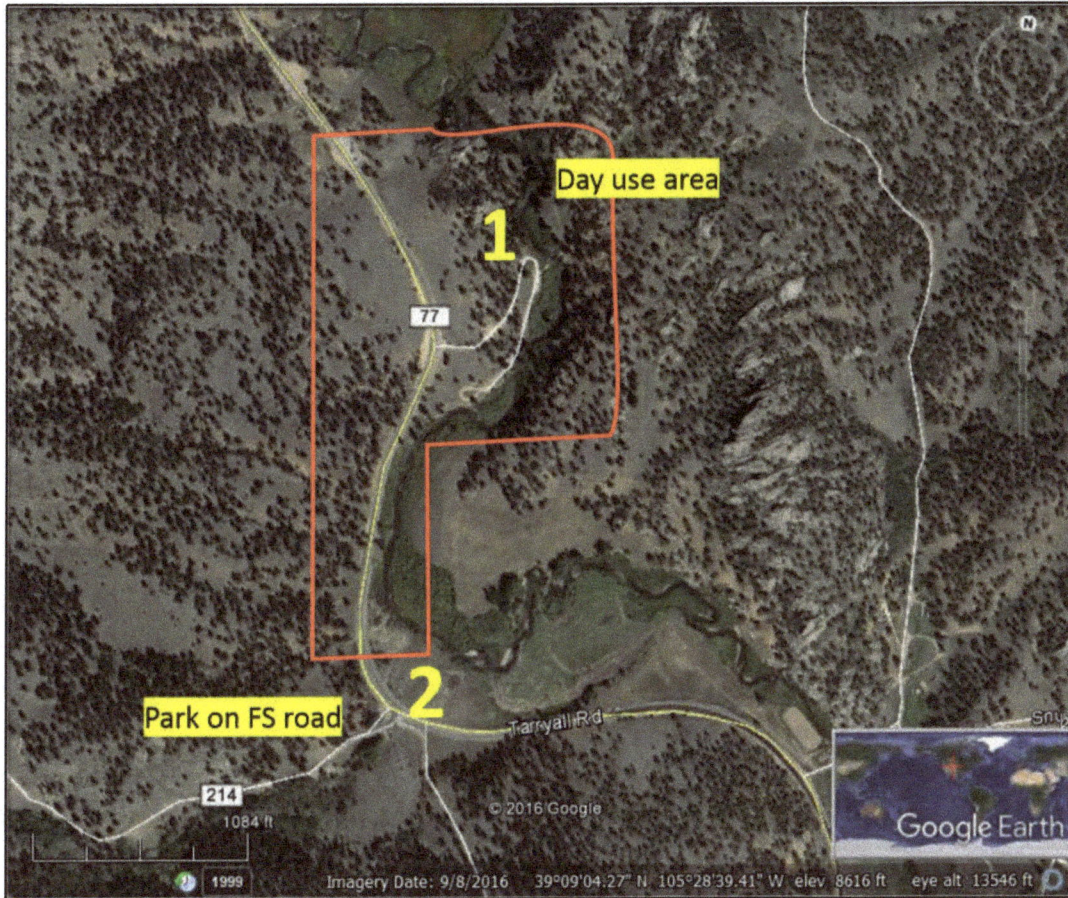

Between mile markers 27 and 26 (mile markers get smaller heading toward Jefferson from Lake George). You can either pay for day use at the **Twin Eagle** picnic area, then park and fish there; or, park on FSR 214 (across from a barren horse pasture, which has large truck tires used for feeding horses). If you park on FSR 214, you can walk across the road to access the river. Signs say, "Closed for restoration" but that means closed to vehicles, not closed to wade fishing.

The picnic day use area has a trail head and a bridge to cross the river. So, this is a great place for people who want to hike on trails in the Lost Creek Wilderness while other people fish. This part of the river is next to the road but it is heavily lined by willows and is seldom fished.

16

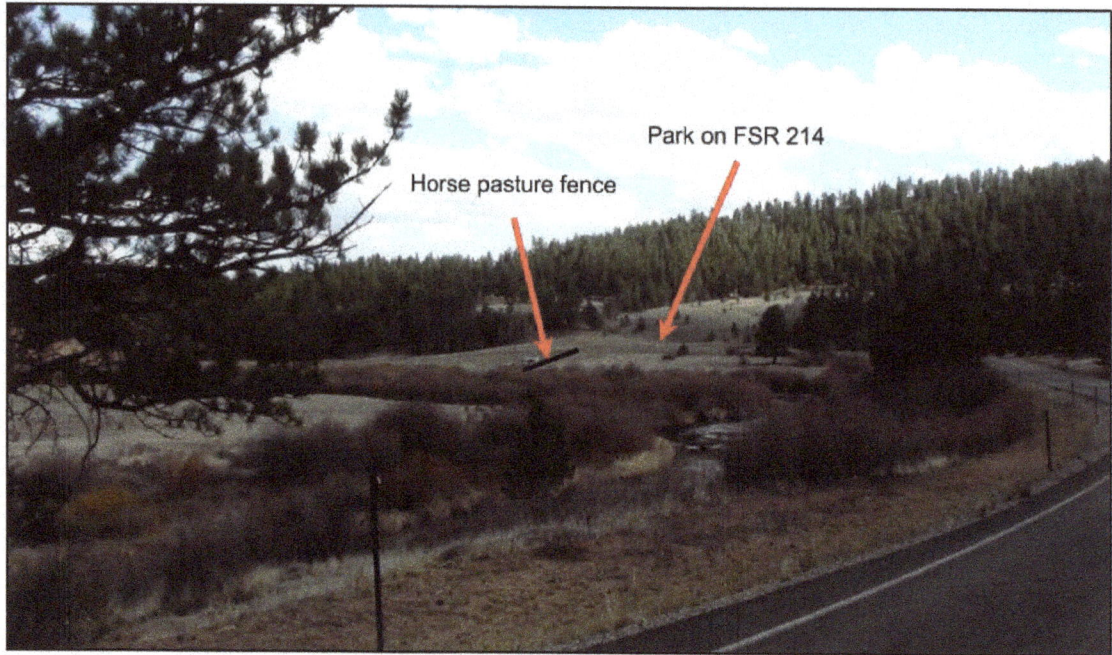

Tarryall River below Twin Eagle Picnic Ground looking downstream toward the horse pasture and FSR 214 parking area. This stretch is seldom fished. Browns hold along the banks. There are riffles and boulders with eddies.

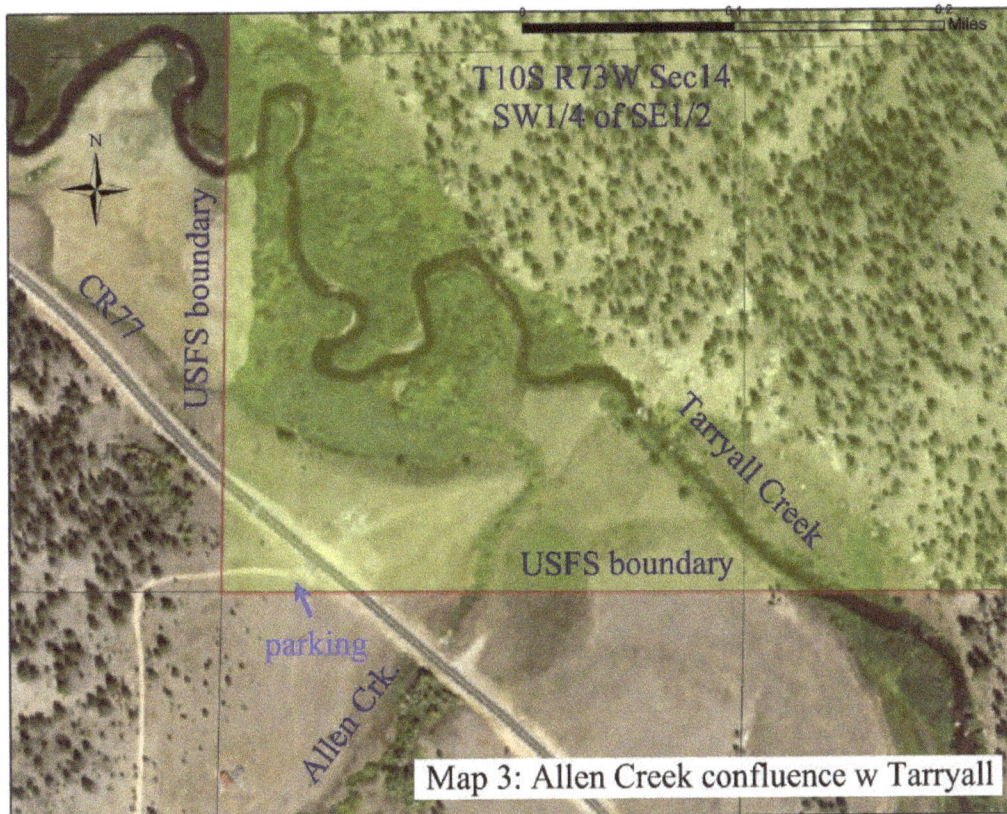

Map 3: Allen Creek confluence w Tarryall

At mile marker 24 continue to the top of the hill, look for a yellow cattle sign like this park at the cattleguard. The easiest way down is to walk along the fence line to the river because the brush is thick and there is a steep cliff between the road and the creek. The oxbows are wide and willow-lined. The water bunches up in a lake behind a cascade (white areas in this photo) and the Tarryall River drops in rapids and pools downstream.

This is moose habitat and there may be beaver ponds (CDOW removes them...)

18

You can find some large trout (18+") here but they are spooky. The cascade stretch is lined by trees, so back casts can be difficult. The oxbows are surrounded by "moosy" ground – boggy with thick willows. So, hiking through the brush is difficult. That said, brown trout (10-14") are in every good hole and numerous smaller trout in the riffles.

Deep wide lakes of water stacked up in oxbows behind the cascades.

The Broadmoor Fishing Resort has a prominent entrance sign seen from the road. Just past that resort is a public parking area on the right. The Broadmoor stocks with large cutthroats (20+ inches) downstream of the public parking area. You can cross a foot bridge at the parking lot and follow a foot path downstream to fish the lower loops on public land adjacent to the Broadmoor. See if you can get a big cutthroat here. There is a lovely hiking trail (Ute Creek Trailhead) here with information kiosks. The trail leads into the Lost Creek Wilderness.

DO NOT CROSS ANY FENCES. PROPERTY BOUNDARY SIGNS MAY BE MISSING.

20

This is the bridge to cross the Tarryall River from the Ute Creek trailhead. Enticing, eh? This is an excellent place for someone to fish while others hike.

There are two outlets at the spillway of Tarryall Reservoir. The cascades hold *abundant* smaller rainbows (9-10"), likely derived from the stocked fish in the reservoir but brown trout and larger rainbows (14-20") hang out in a deep undercut bank at the bend next to the highway. Sometimes, there are pike under the bridge. You will be able to watch abundant trout feeding here but they may be wily.

This is what the water looks like below the spillway at Tarryall Reservoir. Glassy and clear means wily trout. You have to utilize cover.

At the inlet to Tarryall Reservoir, pass the white houses on the right, pass mile marker 16 and then look for green gates on the left. There are two acess points. Park on the shoulder. The gates are unlocked. This inlet holds abundant rainbows, cutthroat, and brown trout of a variety of sizes. The banks are highly incised. The fish will be spooked if you fish from the bank. Get in the water.

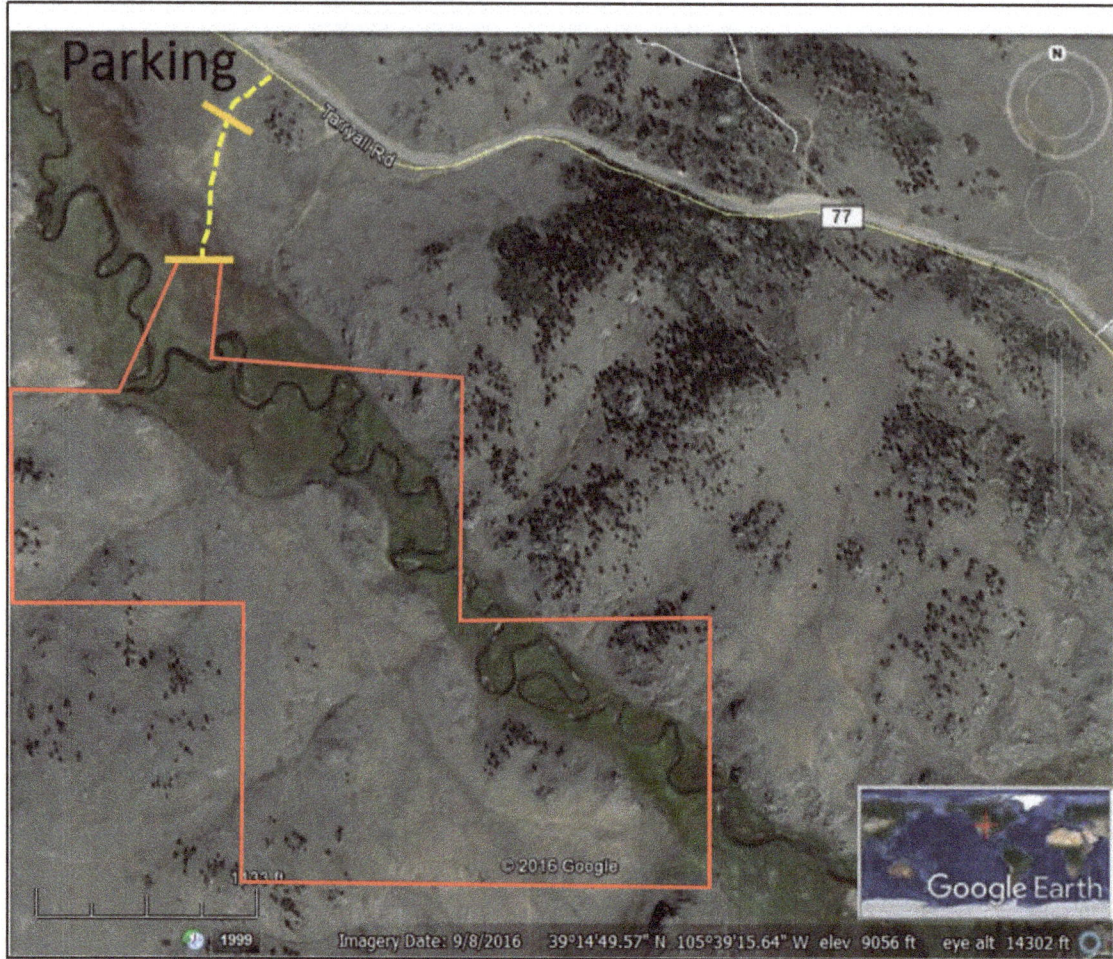

Two miles beyond Tarryall Reservoir go past mile marker "14" and look for a gravel parking area on the left. There is a prominant "No fishing - private club" sign, but that applies only to upstream. There is a Colorado Department of Wildlife Fishing Access sign down the trail. You have to walk through two fences (crow's foot openings in the fences). This is a long stretch of prime river fishing.

This is what the Tarryall looks like at the SWA site.

(Technically this is Michigan Creek - you passed the confluence of Tarryall Creek at the Stagestop Saloon.) At mile marker "6" there are 2 historic log buildings on the right and then a parking area with information kiosks on the left. The river both downstream and upstream (across the road) is public access, though it is fenced off. Upstream access is fenced with barbed wire but you can cross using a blanket over the wire. Public access upstream goes around the bend to the left but not all the way to the highway. Stay to the right to continue fishing upstream. The last 100'of river before the highway is private and is fenced off. That said, the best habitat is a boulder-lined canyon in the first bend. There are large 18+ inch brown trout in there. You can also fish downstream to the lower fenceline.

LOST CREEK WILDERNESS

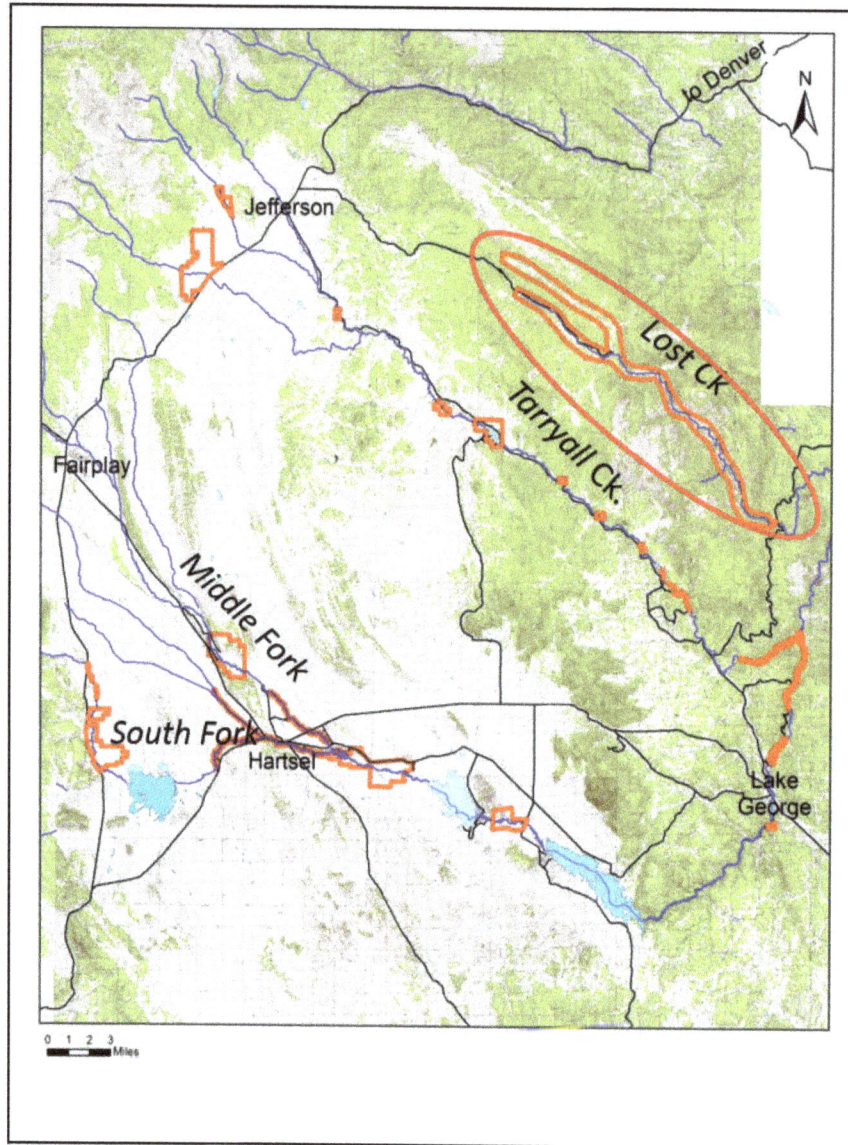

Map: Overview of the Lost Creek Wilderness Area.

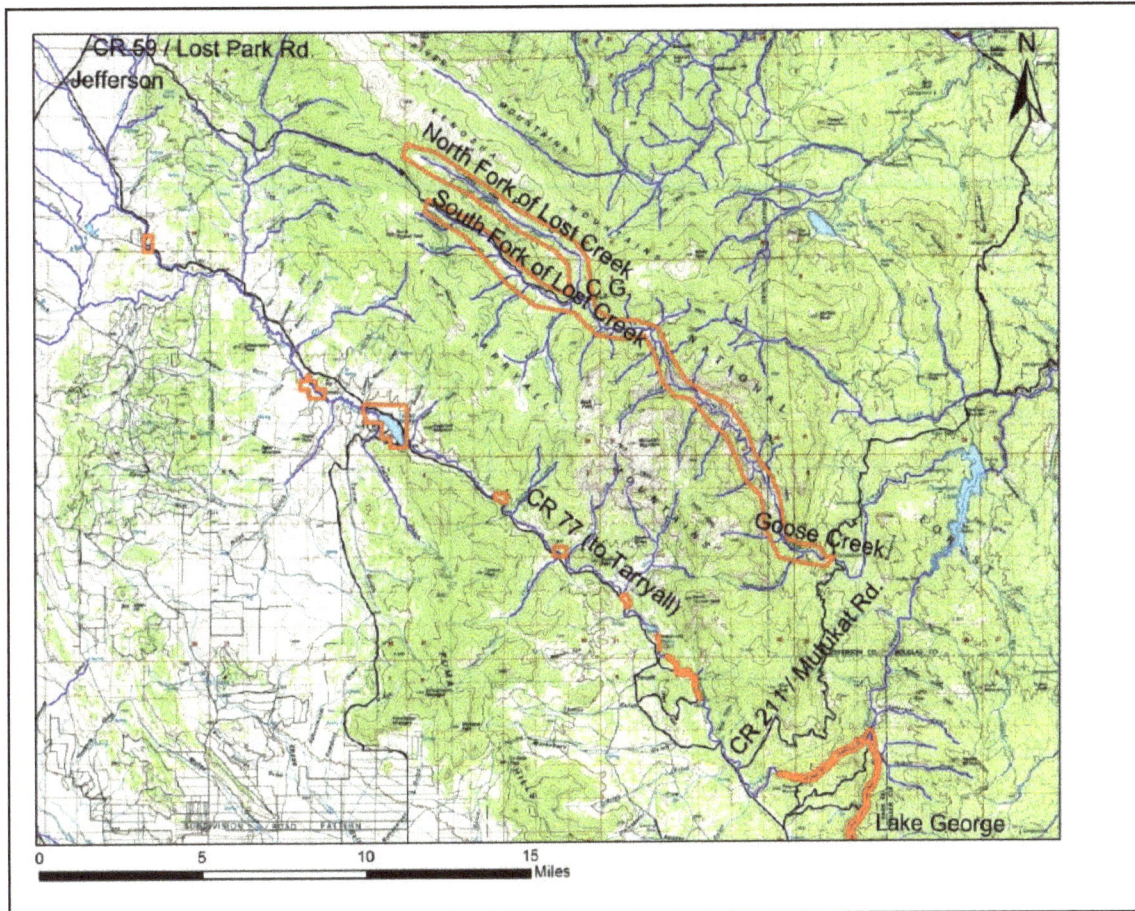

Lost Creek is a small stream chock full of brookies. You can have a 100+-fish day there (I have). It is an excellent venue for Tenkara or a small rod. There are two forks of Lost Creek (which is called Goose Creek in Jefferson County). The North Fork and South Forks of Lost Creek are both fishable, though really narrow and bound by thick currant, rose, berry and willow bushes. The volume of water increases at their confluence into a narrow but deep channel varying from 3 to 8 feet across with pools, islands, channel bars and undercut banks. There are also beaver ponds, which are full of spooky fish. It's easy to walk alongside Lost Creek except in the vicinity of the beaver ponds, which make walking difficult.

Lost Creek about 5 miles downstream from the confluence of the two forks.

There are two ways to access this stream. Either drive to the **Lost Creek Campground** from the west, or drive to the **Goose Creek Trailhead** from the east. You will see a lot of hikers at the east Goose Creek end because it is a convenient drive from Denver. The Goose Creek end also drains into Chatfield Reservoir, which is why there are errant rainbows or browns on the east end.

Route from the WEST: One mile north of Jefferson, turn onto CR 56 / Lost Park Road. This dirt road ends in 20 miles at Lost Park Campground. Drive through the campground on the left to access a day use parking area. You can also park and fish the South Fork of Lost Creek along the way.

Route from the EAST: from Lake George: turn onto CR77. Take a right onto CR 211 (Mutakat Rd.) Go 16 more miles to Goose Creek Trailhead. This road (Mutakat) continues on to Deckers.

TOMAHAWK

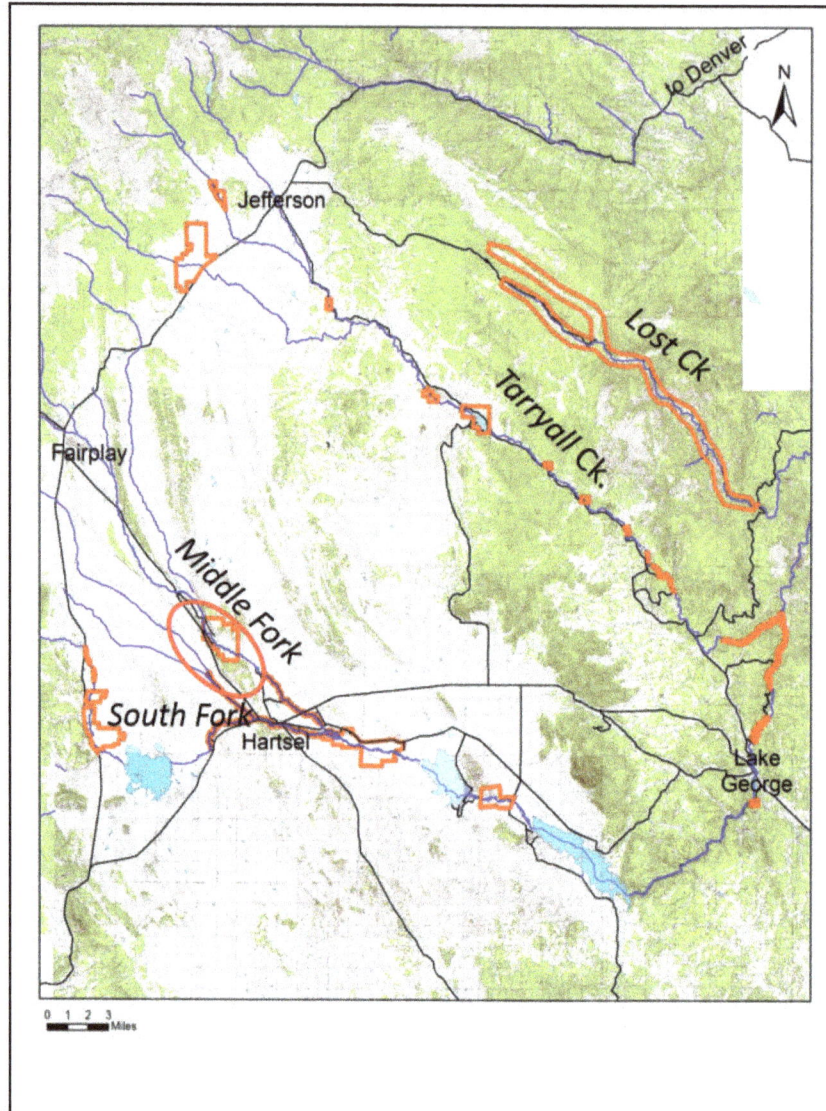

Tomahawk is a State Wildlife Area (SWA) for access to the Middle Fork of the South Platte. It's known for braided meanders, oxbows, riffles, and deep pools.

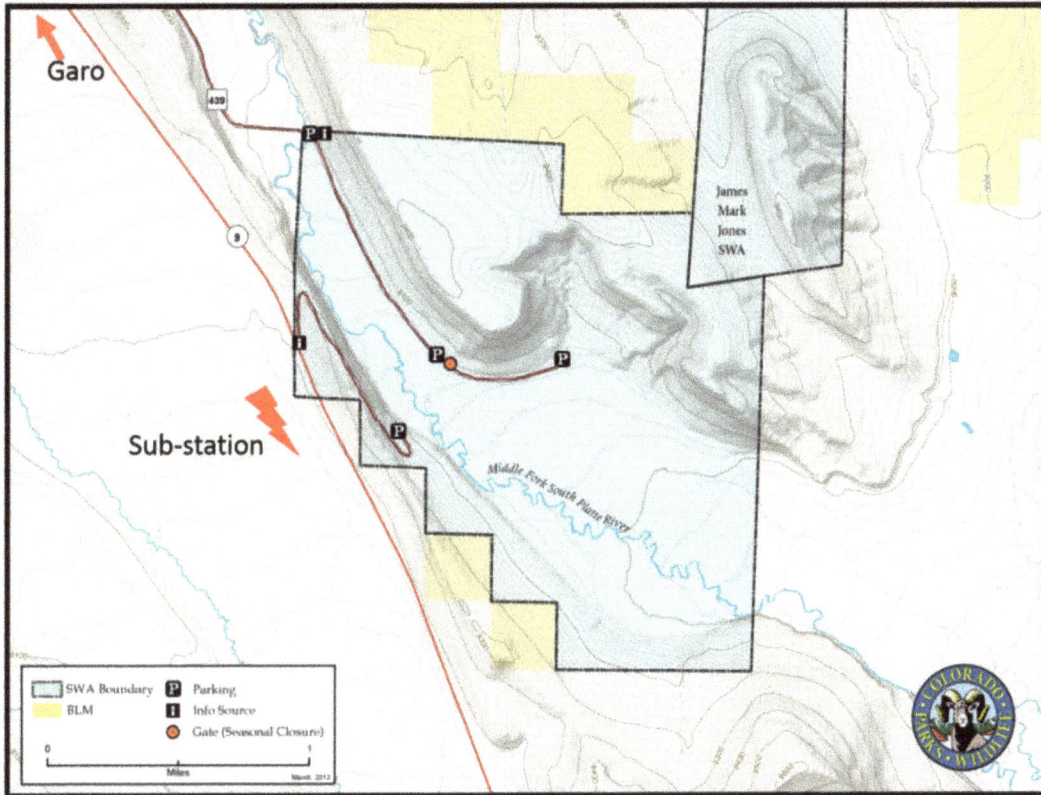

Tomahawk State Wildlife Area

TOMAHAWK ACCESS OPTION 1

This is a steep hike. From Hartsel going toward Fairplay on Hwy 9 look for a "Colorado State Parks and Wildlife" sign up the ridge on the right just after an **electrical sub-station** (5 miles from the Hwy 24 / Hwy 9 turn off). This dirt road leads to a parking area on a ridge overlooking the river. It's a steep walk to get down to the river but the ridge is the best way to walk downstream because the valley bottom is thick with vegetation and beaver channels. Larger trout size increases as you go downstream but it is difficult walking.

TOMAHAWK ACCESS OPTION 2

Easier access. Pass by the first access and continue on to **Garo** (a junction with an old mercantile building on the left and a large, 2-story wooden compound on the right). Just past these buildings is a right turn that follows the Middle Fork to two parking areas on the lower plain of Tomahawk. (BTW – Garo is no longer public access, though you may see cars there.)

Tomahawk (below) is fed by wild Trout Creek upstream and is adjacent to the Santa Maria Fishing Resort downstream. There are lots of braided meanders, islands, riffles, holes, and channels to choose from. The trout are predominantly wild brown trout varying in size from 7 inches and up. There is no limit on how big the lunkers can get as this is such a varied trout habitat. This is a good place to spread out if you have a group of people.

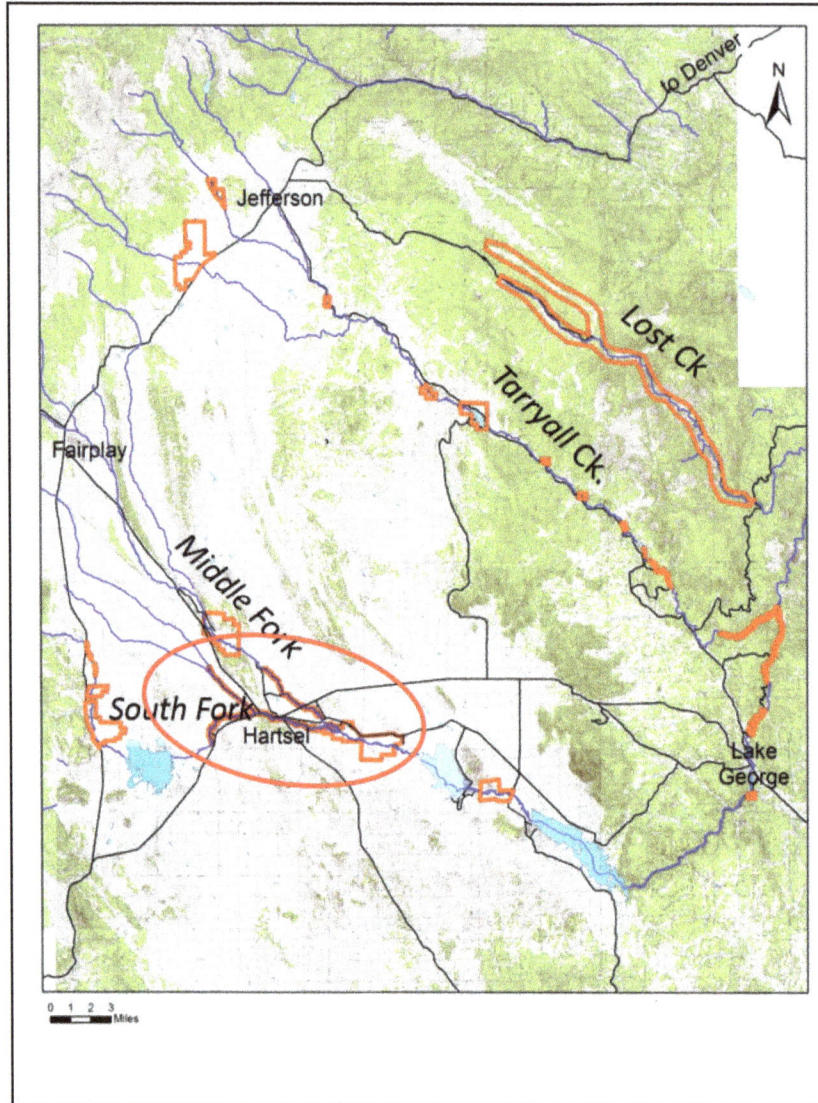

River access above Spinney Reservoir – a confluence zone of multiple tributaries of the South Platte River in the vicinity of Hartsel.

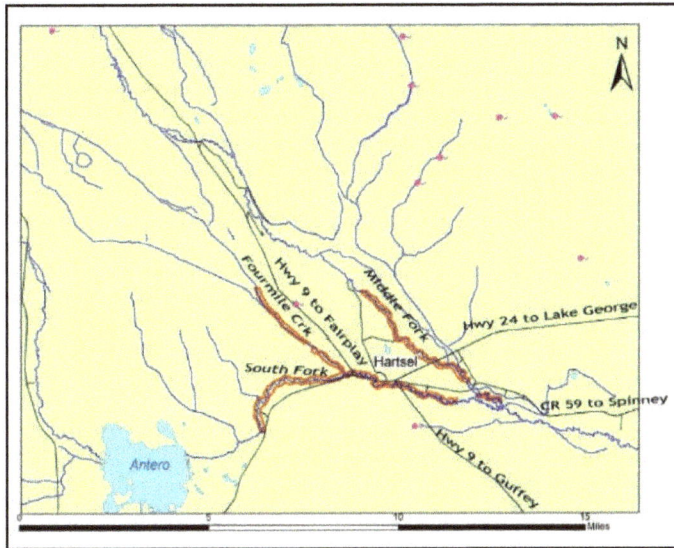

Three tributaries (South Fork, Fourmile Crk., Middle Fork) feed the South Platte near Hartsel.

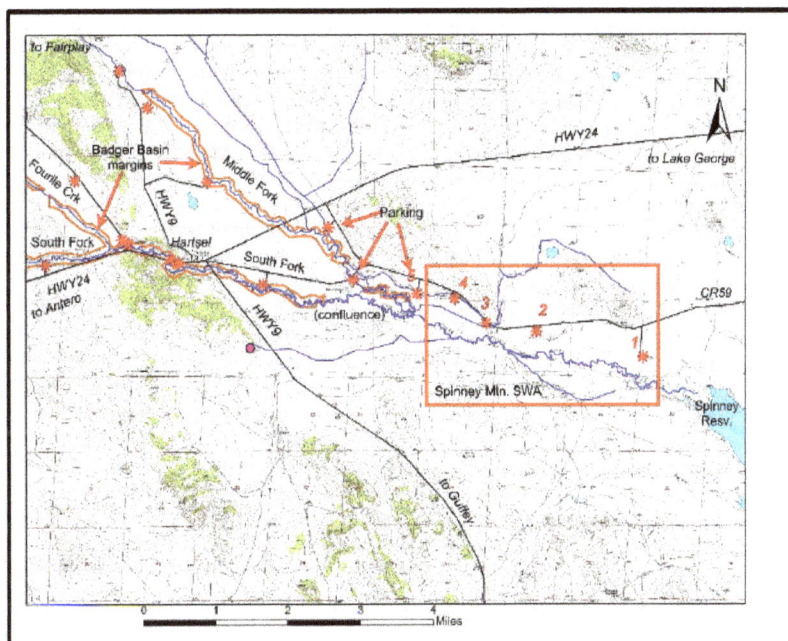

Dots = free parking access to the South Platte River. Red box = Spinney Mtn. SWA above the reservoir. Red margins are portions of the South Platte within Badger Basin SWA.

(Across from a historic white "I-house"). This is a long walk from parking to the water. You can access the inlet to Spinney Reservoir for pike fishing here. The river holds browns and rainbows as well. You can access Spinney on foot from here if it is legally open.

Jerome and Viola Harrington's historic "I-House", 1876, at access 1.

This is another long walk to the water from the parking area. This part of the river has thick willow patches, which make for good trout habitat.

The predominant wild trout species in the South Platte River is brown trout about 12-16" average with a chance to get a true lunker of 20+ inches or even a pike or rainbow. The river makes oxbows through a wide-open hay valley. Terrestrials are a good pattern in the summer, especially on a windy day. Solitude!

This is a simple roadside pullout. Walk through hay fields to the water. There are ruins of an old bridge (Colorado Midland Railway) on the river here.

The predominant species here is brown trout about 12-16" average with a chance to get a true lunker of 18+ inches or even a pike or rainbow.

Hard to see from the road because it is inside the premise of the historic Baker's Ranch hay buildings and bunk houses. It is a BIG parking lot.

This access is a moderate walk through hay fields to willow-lined oxbows with riffles and undercut banks. You can access the confluence from area here. The predominant species is brown trout about 12-16" average with a chance to get a true lunker of 18+ inches or even a pike or rainbow.

This is the first access in Badger Basin SWA. A fence / cattle guard separates Spinney Mtn. SWA from Badger Basin SWA. This accesses the heart of the confuence area. (DETAILS IN THE NEXT CHAPTER)

South Park is open range to a variety of domestic stock including cattle, burros and horses. You might also see wild bison, pronghorn, elk, badger, coyotes as well as ducks, geese, blue herons, hawks, eagles, and osprey. A local rancher also has beef-a-lo (cow-bison cross) - some of which are white. He also has yaks, European deer, elk and lamas.

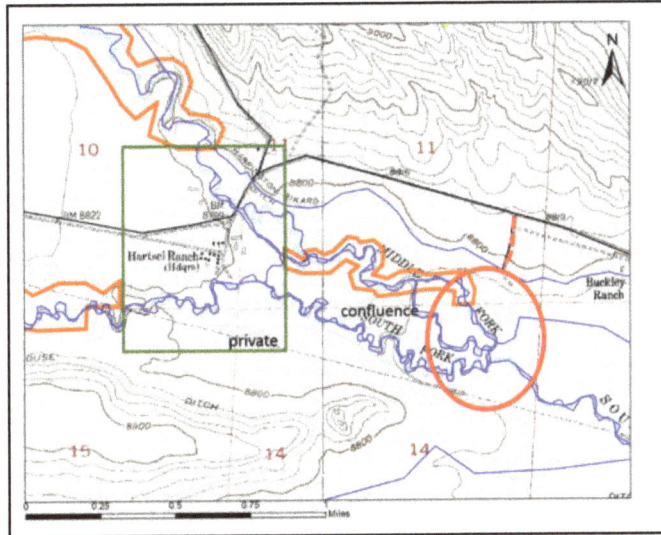

Badger Basin at the confluence is downstream of the Hartsel Springs private ranch. Look for CPW SWA sign and parking before crossing a cattle guard

The Confluence of the Middle Fork and South Fork below the Hartsel Springs Ranch is a *ZONE* rather than a well-defined junction. There are many meanders and islands with complex hydraulic characteristics, which make for rewarding fishing.

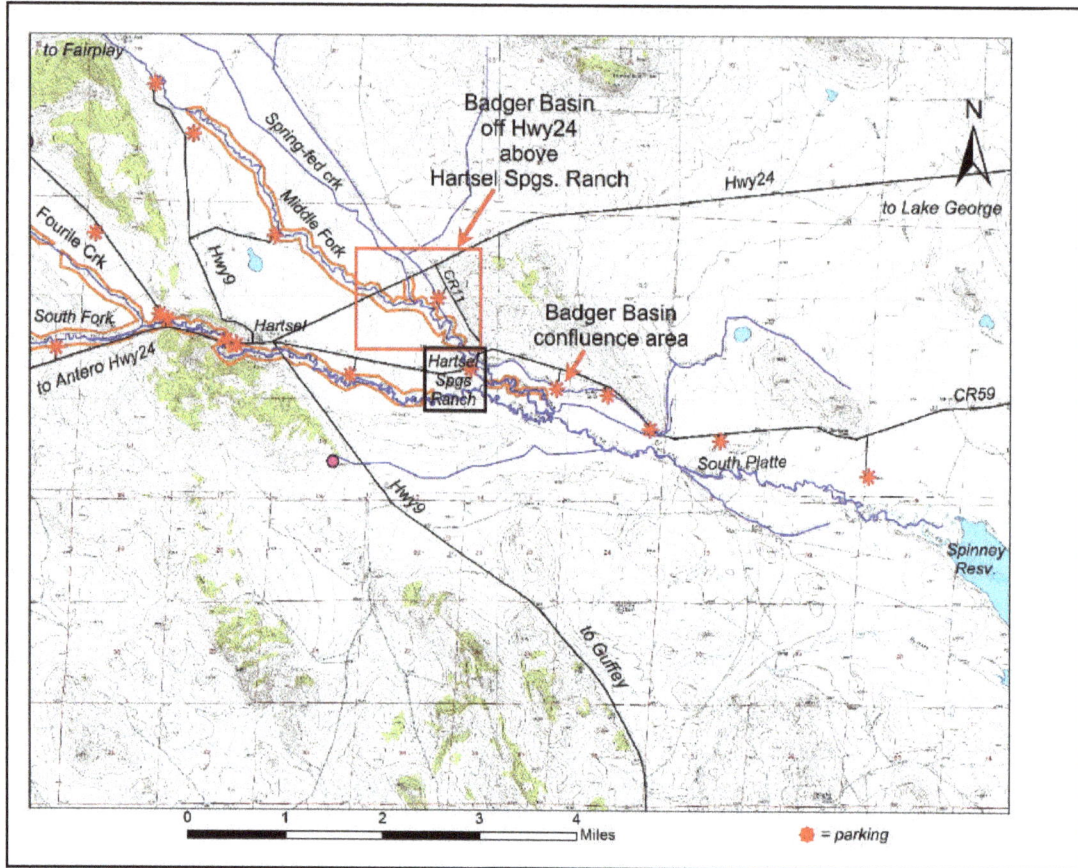

Badger Basin: The Middle Fork between Hwy 24 and Hartsel Springs Ranch provides access to two bodies of fishable water – the main channel of the Middle Fork and a wild spring-fed stream that feeds into the Middle Fork only here. The Middle Fork at this access runs through a heavily-grazed pasture but the extents of public access go past the fence line both upstream and downstream, which includes one big bend against a steep cliff with undercut banks. There are tight oxbows, channel bars, and islands. No willows.

Directions From Lake George: About 23 miles, Highway 24 starts to dropdown into a valley right before Hartsel. Almost a full mile past mile marker 242, there is a left turn onto a dirt road (CR11). Turn there to see the parking lot.

Badger Basin parking on the Middle between Hwy 24 and Hartsel Ranch.

This is the wild spring-fed creek that holds trout during spring run-off.

This is the Middle Fork during spring run-off at this access.

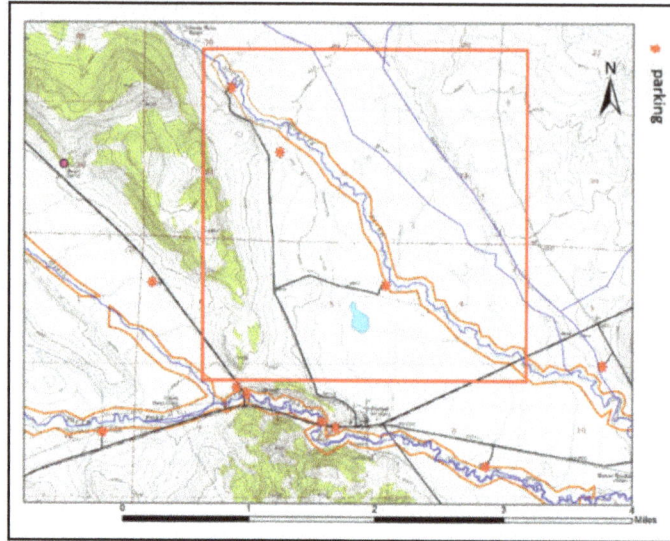

Badger Basin: The Middle Fork *north* of Hwy 24 (between Hartsel and Tomahawk) has 3 access areas. Turn at the gas station in Hartsel onto Mariposa Street. Take the first left onto CR 439 (at an old green shack - this looks like a private driveway but it is a county road). Of the 3 access areas, the last one is wheelchair accessible (shown below). The character of the Middle Fork in this vicinity is wide, flat loops of relatively uniform water with intermittent riffles and undercut banks. You can wade alone with a dog all day on this section of river. The brown trout on the surface are small (8-10") and easy to catch. Lunkers reside in undercuts and deep holes. This part of the river system is highly underutilized.

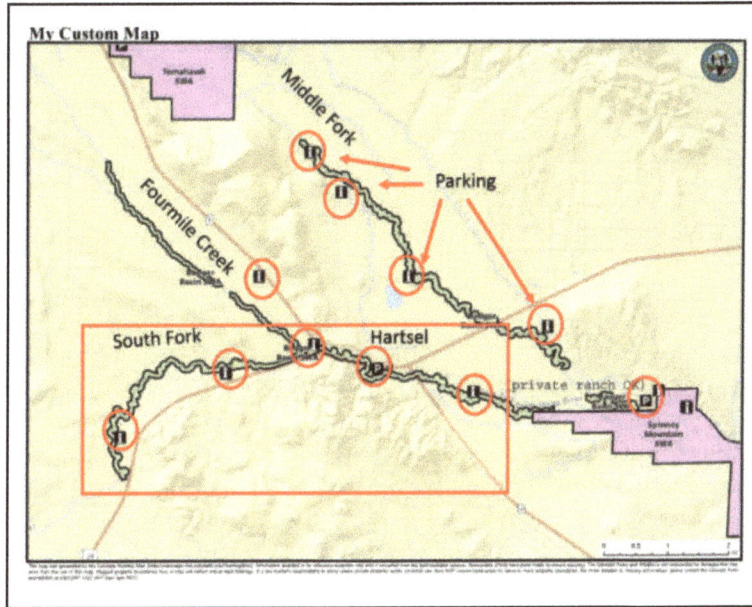

My Custom Map

Badger Basin: The South Fork of the South Platte is public fishing access for its entire length between the westernmost parking lot near Antero, eastward through Hartsel, down to the Hartsel Springs Ranch. There are multiple places to pull off the road and park on the shoulder to fish, such as at this green gate across from the west end of town in Hartsel.

View looking west on Hwy 24 toward the end of town. Park on the shoulder. The river flows behind the rocky hill on the left out of view. The hot springs water is not favorable for trout but upstream or downstream of the hot springs is fine. There are always brown trout in the South Fork.

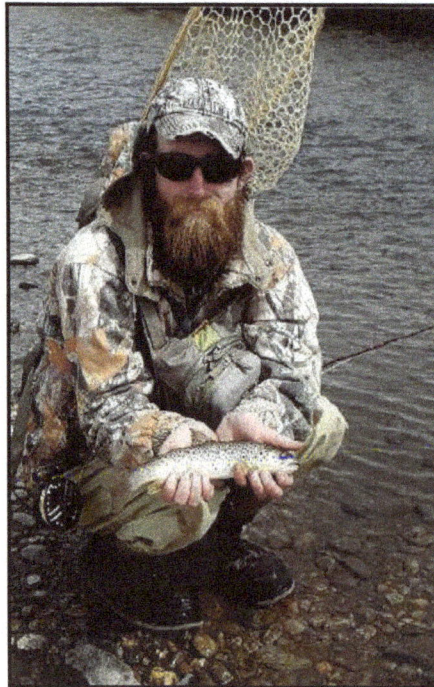

There is an obvious parking area on both sides of Hwy 9 (the turn off to Fairplay). That part of the South Fork of the South Platte is only intermittently profitable. It can get really low, warm and weedy. The Denver Water Board (DWB) controls the discharge from Antero Reservoir. They currently do not allow levels to sustain trout at the tailwaters of Antero year-round. That is an ongoing debate between fish people and the DWB. If the volume of discharge could sustain trout year-round (like Spinney and Eleven Mile), then Antero could become another viable gold medal tailwater. (*sigh*)

This is South Fork of South Platte at the junction of Hwy 24 and Hwy 9. There are parking areas on both sides of the highway. This is a view looking downstream toward Hartsel. The temperature and oxygen level fluctuates rapidly. You can park on the shoulder and look for rising trout to know if it is a good time to fish here.

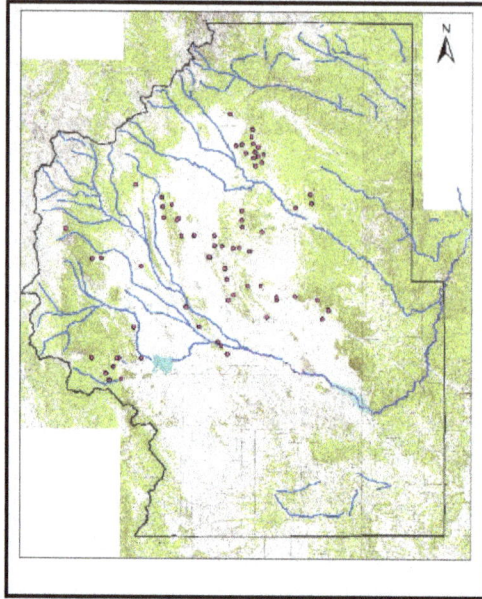

Springs in South Park:

Just why would you want to fish here? Because the South Fork is recharged by springs. There are 70+ springs in South Park (above) contributing cool water enriched in organic material for aquatic insects. The South Fork can hold giant trout (+20 inches) when the rest of the river is blown out by during spring run-off. During spawn, trout migrate up the South Fork to enter the small wild creeks. Pods of trout show up then leave and then return again rather unpredictably in the South Fork.

There are three parking areas on Hwy 24 to fish between Hartsel and Antero. They are lined by tall wire fences to keep the bison in and they have large SWA signs at the end of the drive like this:

NOTE: Real dangers include wild bison or quicksand. Watch for bison and wade on firm ground.

BADGER BASIN: FOURMILE CREEK

Within a mile after turning onto Hwy 9 from Hwy 24 headed for Fairplay from Hartsel, you might notice a well-marked parking area on the left at the end of an aisle of high-wire fencing. That is the Fourmile Creek fishing access of Badger Basin.

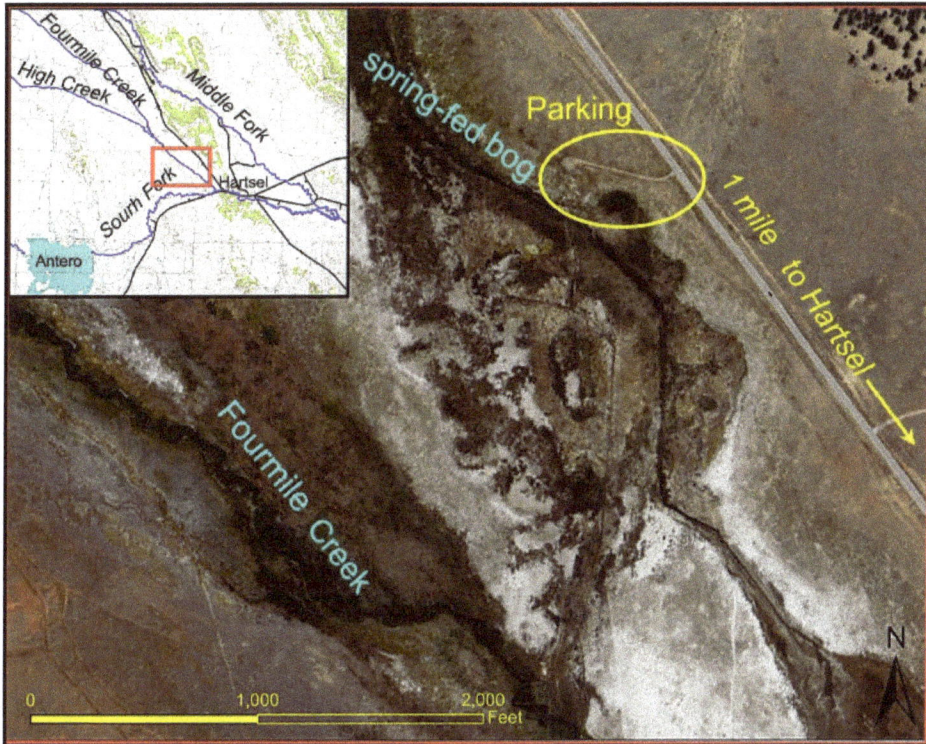

NEVER ENTER A PASTURE WHEN BISON ARE PRESENT!

Directions from Hartsel: go west on Hwy 24 to the turn off to Fairplay (Hwy 9). Take a right on Hwy 9 and continue for 1 mile. Look for the parking access on the left. Walking from the parking area you first cross a boggy spring fed creek that is NOT Fourmile Creek. Keep going. Fourmile creek is about 2,000 feet further after a difficult trudge over lumpy bumpy ground and maybe accompanied by black biting flies due to bison and horse dung. The creek is lined with long buffalo grass and mostly obscured from view until you are upon it. It is about 8-15 feet wide, cobble bottom, riffles, undercuts, eddies and intermittent downed fence posts. The smaller trout feed on the surface and lunkers hold in undercuts and in deep holes. Multiple spring-fed creeks run into Fourmile Creek, which has its origin in Mosquito Range.

Wild springs feed High Creek, which flows into Fourmile Creek out in the middle of South Park basin. Fourmile Creek is recharged by run-off and spring water, which is why it hosts wild trout.

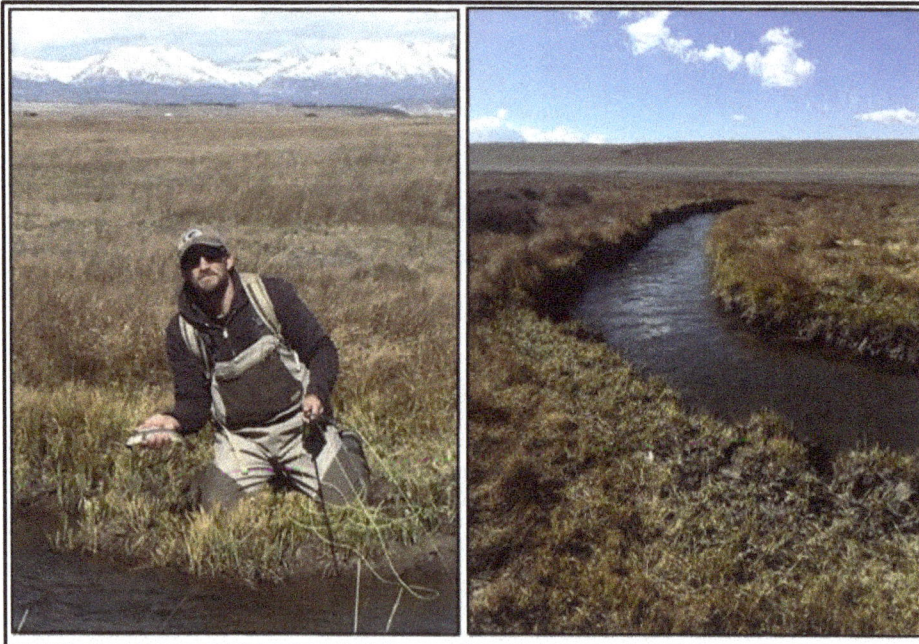

WILD HEADWATERS

WILD HEADWATERS:

- Jefferson Creek / Lake
- Teter-Michigan Creek SWA
- Cline Ranch SWA
- Knight Imler / 63 Ranch
- Rough and Tumbling Creek

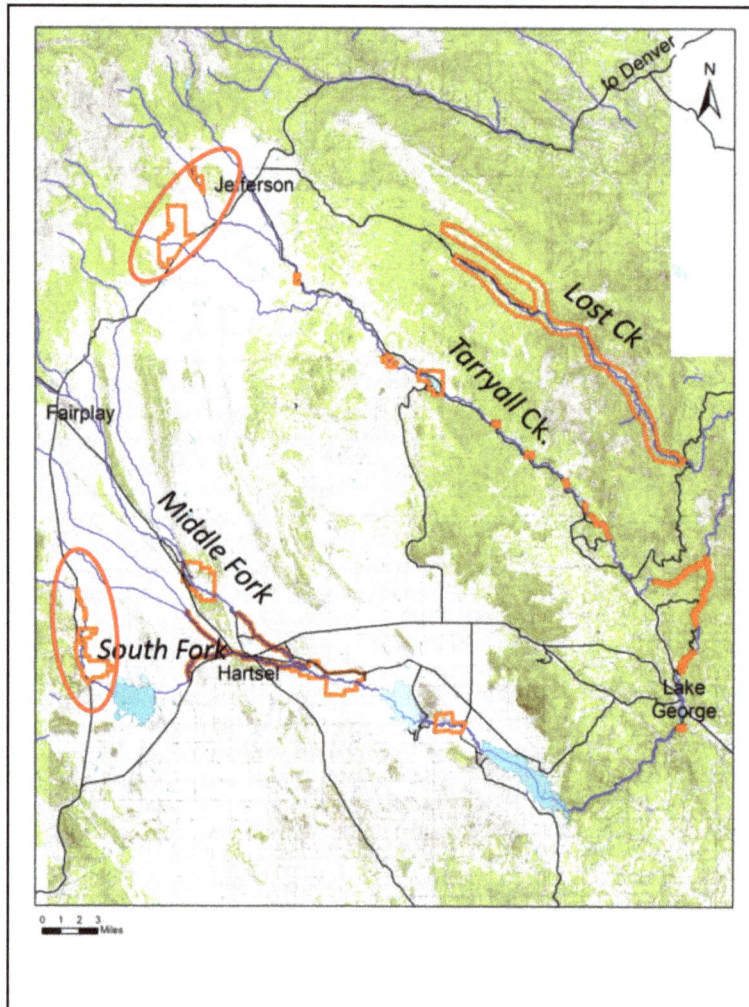

Jefferson Creek & Lake, Teter-Michigan Creek SWA, and Tarryall Creek (Cline SWA), are all accessed off Hwy 285 between Como and Jefferson.

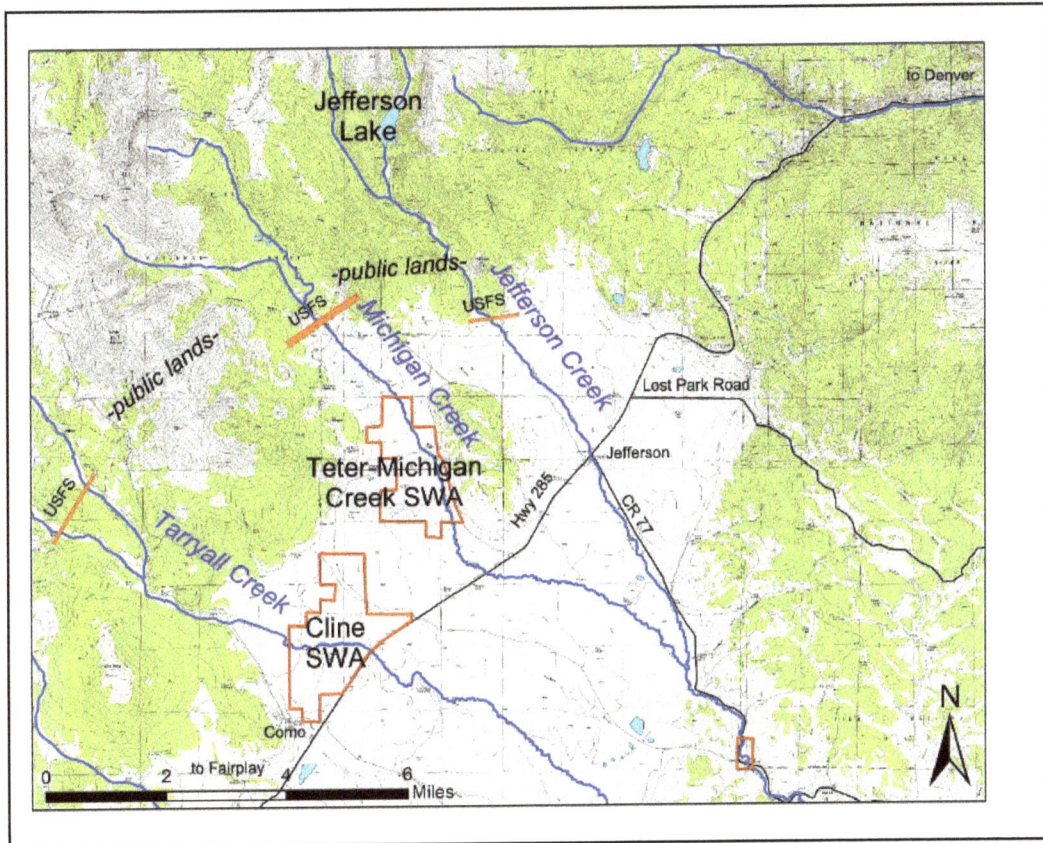

All three of these creeks originate in the USFS and can be accessed either in SWA parking areas and also by USFS public lands upstream. These are my favorite streams for some local fall cast-n-blast expeditions - grouse, doves, ducks, turkey and trout!

56

JEFFERSON CREEK (AND JEFFERSON LAKE)

This area is 5 miles west of Jefferson. Take CR 35 west, turn right onto CR 37. The lake (May – Oct.) holds rainbow, brown, mackinaw, and brook trout. The tailwaters and creek can be really low in the summer with best fishing in fall when the browns migrate. You have to pay a $7 fee to get into the park to fish the tailwaters. It is loaded with moose here, too.

The Lake

The Creek

Also located on CR 35, (which forms a loop around Michigan Hill going from Hwy 285 in Jefferson back to Hwy 285 about 2 miles south of Jefferson). Michigan Creek is known for abundant smaller trout of a variety of species – browns, rainbow, cutthroat and brookies.

THE CLINE RANCH (TARRYALL CREEK)

Cline Ranch is the headwaters of the Tarryall River. It holds larger (12 - 16") rainbows and brown trout, especially upstream toward the beaver ponds. There are 4 parking areas, assigned to 4 beats. The upper 2 beats are parallel forks of the Tarryall and are ponded behind beaver dams. I walk the channels downstream of the dams to fish the deep pools.

KNIGHT IMLER AND 63 RANCH SWA

These access the South Fork of the South Platte River above Antero Reservoir. Knight Imler has two parking areas and 63 Ranch has three on Hwy 285 between Antero and Fairplay. They are contiguous. Look for CPW signs between mile markers 168 and 169.

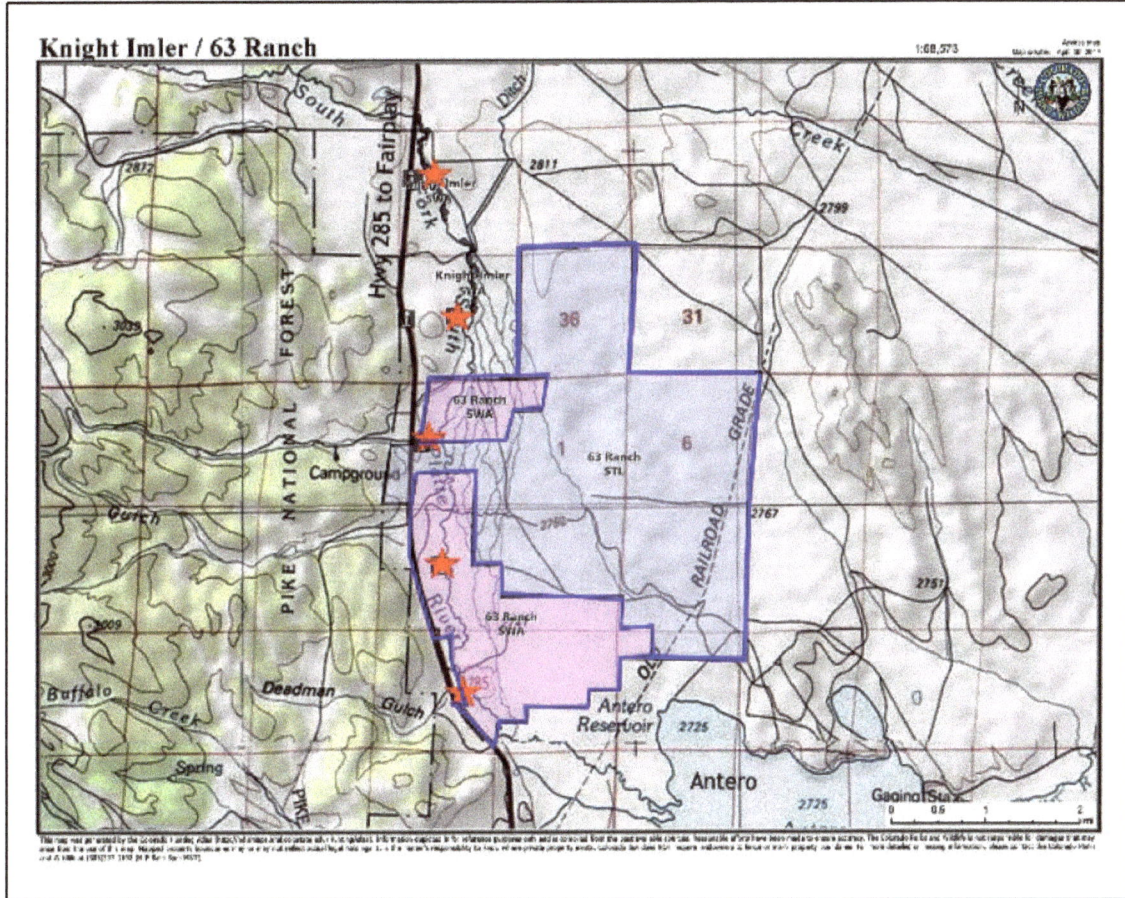

Knight Imler / 63 Ranch

63 Ranch offers public fishing access along the river through the middle of an operating cattle ranch. Fences keep the cattle off the river. There are riffles, undercut banks and drops into deep holes. The majority of fish are 8-12" browns and rainbows but there are extraordinarily large brown trout in some of the larger holes and back eddies. This portion of the South Platte is the closest you can get to the inlet of Antero.

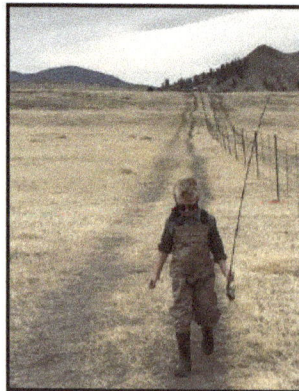

THE KNIGHT IMLER

Knight Imler SWA is easy to see from Hwy 285 because the sign is close to the highway and there is a large canvas hut there. This is a riffly creek with bends and drops, lots of willows – roll-casting is a must.

A "fen"…

Of significance to Knight Imler and South Park in general, are the Pleistocene-age fens (ancient bogs seen above). There are 24 fens in South Park between Antero and Kenosha Pass. These bogs are protected because they host globally unique species of plants and animals.

Knight Imler SWA is lined by willows and wild grass. There are riffles and undercut banks.

ROUGH AND TUMBLING CREEK

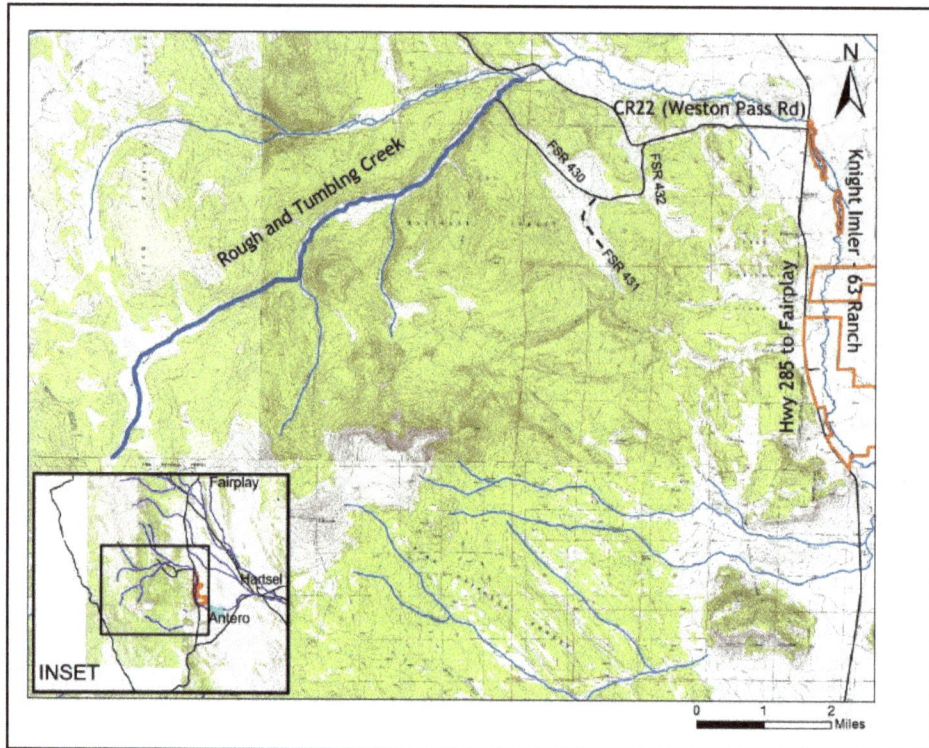

Rough and Tumbling Creek is the headwaters of the South Fork. It flows out of the Mosquito Range and is accessed via CR 22 – Weston Pass Road - across from Knight Imler. Take CR 22 west for 2 miles; take a left on FSR 432 over a cattle guard; continue over a second cattle guard; stay right at a fork onto FSR 430. Either cross the creek in 4WD or hike upstream. Most roadside access at the stream is steep but there are flat areas at stream crossings, where you can also camp. The wading is difficult through brush and around beaver ponds. This creek can hold large (16-18") rainbows, native cuts, and brown trout as well as boodles of brookies.

The dirt road that leads to Rough and Tumbling Creek goes through public lands that allow dispersed camping but the road becomes rutted and narrow close to the creek. The stream crossings require 4WD to get up the bank but there are flat areas at the stream crossings large enough to make camp.

Rough and Tumbling Creek at the first stream crossing.

Author's Biography

Michele White is a retired geologist and bassoonist. She is currently a Certified Professional Fly Fishing Guide and owner of Tumbling Trout Fly Shop in Lake George, Colorado. In 1998, she transitioned from kayaking and rafting on the Colorado River to rowing a dory and fly fishing the great rivers of the west under her husband's guidance. Doug White, (her husband, aka, "*The Bun*"), is also an avid fly fisher and geologist. Michele is a contributing editor for Mountain Gazette, (thanks to John Fayhee), and has been published in *Discover the Outdoors, EQUUS, Fly Fishing World, Native People's Magazine, New Tribal Dawn*, and *The Aquarian*.

Her books include:

- "Joe Schmo Can Catch a Big Fish", self-published, 2020.
- "Between the Rivers", with co-authors Al Marlowe and Karen Rae Christopherson, 2019.
- "*Lesser Known Fly Fishing Venues in South Park, Colorado*", self-published, 2016;
- "*Eulogies and Dead Horses*", self-published, 2016;
- "*Colorado Mountain Dogs*", published by WestWinds Press - The Pruett Series, an imprint of Graphic Arts Books, 2014;
- "*Comeback Wolves: Western Writers Speak for Wolves in the Southern Rockies*", published by Johnson Books, 2005; and
- "*Hell's Half Mile: River Runners' Tales of Hilarity and Misadventure*", published by Breakaway Books, 2004.

Thank you,

Michele White
V.P. Education, Pikes Peak Chapter of Trout Unlimited
Tumbling Trout Fly Shop

www.tumblingtrout.com

mwhite@tumblingtrout.com or Aubassoon@aol.com
720.363.2092 (mobile)

38283 Hwy 24
Lake George, CO 80827
·´¯`·.,,..><((((º>·´¯`·.,,..><((((º>·´¯`·.,,..><((((º>

www.ingramcontent.com/pod-product-compliance
Lightning Source LLC
Chambersburg PA
CBHW042354030426
42336CB00029B/3474